Ten S[...]
Poen[...]

ex libris

Candlestick Press

Published by:

Candlestick Press,

Diversity House, 72 Nottingham Road, Arnold, Nottingham UK NG5 6LF

www.candlestickpress.co.uk

Design and typesetting by Diversity Creative Marketing Solutions Ltd.,
www.diversity.agency

Printed by Ratcliff & Roper Print Group, Nottinghamshire, UK

Selection and Introduction © Di Slaney, 2018

Cover illustration © Woman from Baku/Shutterstock

Candlestick Press monogram © Barbara Shaw, 2008

© Candlestick Press, 2018

ISBN 978 1 907598 69 2

Acknowledgements:

The poems in this pamphlet are reprinted from the following books, all by
permission of the publishers listed unless stated otherwise. Every effort has
been made to trace the copyright holders of the poems published in this
book. The editor and publisher apologise if any material has been included
without permission or without the appropriate acknowledgement, and
would be glad to be told of anyone who has not been consulted. Thanks are
due to all the copyright holders cited below for their kind permission:

Kim Addonizio, *Tell Me*. Copyright © 2000 by Kim Addonizio. Reprinted
with the permission of The Permissions Company, Inc., on behalf of BOA
Editions, Ltd., www.boaeditions.org

Jo Bell, *Navigation* (Moormaid Press, 2014)

Wayne Burrows, *The Apple Sequence* (Orchard Editions, 2011) by kind
permission of the author.

Hilary Davies, *The Shanghai Owner of the Bonsai Shop* (Enitharmon,
1991) by kind permission of the author.

MR Peacocke, *Caliban Dancing* (Shoestring Press, 2011)

Shazea Quraishi, *The Art of Scratching* (Bloodaxe Books, 2015)
www.bloodaxebooks.com

Neil Rollinson, *A Spillage of Mercury* (Jonathan Cape, 1996)

Anne Sexton, *Complete Poems* (Houghton Mifflin, 1999) by permission of
Sterling Lord Literistic.

James Sheard, *The Abandoned Settlements* (Jonathan Cape, 2017)

All permissions cleared courtesy of Swift Permissions
(swiftpermissions@gmail.com)

Where poets are no longer living, their dates are given.

Contents

Page

Introduction	*Di Slaney*	*5*
Scent	*James Sheard*	*7*
The Ecstasy of St Saviour's Avenue	*Neil Rollinson*	*8*
December 11th	*Anne Sexton*	*9*
For Desire	*Kim Addonizio*	*10*
The Shipwright's Love Song	*Jo Bell*	*11*
Ramadasi	*Shazea Quraishi*	*12*
Hidden Rose	*Wayne Burrows*	*13*
A Kiss Remembered	*MR Peacocke*	*14*
Gloire de Dijon	*DH Lawrence*	*15*
This Morning the Postboy Brought Me a Letter	*Hilary Davies*	*16*

Introduction

What is a sexy poem? A poem that depicts the nature of the
act, or a poem that suggests the heat of the action? 'Both' is,
I suppose, the answer. But in this selection the poems focus
on the latter – language which mimics the slow pulse and
languorous stroke of physical love, as well as its urgency. No
surprise then that within these ten short poems, we take an
intense journey of the senses – the evocative smells and tastes of
love, the thrilling touch and shudder, the overwhelming stimulus
of sight and the cumulative impact of sound. Amazing to find so
many poets using wonderful natural metaphors of bees, apples
(that ancient symbol of temptation) and roses to paint erotic
word pictures for us.

These poems aim to make us a little warmer, a little more tingly,
a little more responsive to desire in all its 'force and splendour'
as MR Peacocke so aptly describes. Find a snug spot to read
them. Find someone lovely to read them with, or to. And find
yourself, even as you sink down into your pillows and disappear
within these pages…

Di Slaney

Scent

The past is there
like a scent, armfuls
of it, arches of it,
lifted, steadied hips
of it, all the rolling
lilting movement of all
of it, fresh clay
of the skin and
the smell of home
in the hair. It is
a casket, split open
and then
closed to me
again.

James Sheard

The Ecstasy of St Saviour's Avenue
(Valentine's Night)

Tonight the tenement smells of oysters
and semen, chocolate and rose petals.
The windows of every flat are open
to cool us, the noise of our limberings
issues from every sash as if the building
was hyperventilating in the cold
February air. We can hear the moans
of the Rossiters, the Hendersons,
the babysitters in number 3; a gentle
pornography rousing us like an aphrodisiac.
For once the house is harmonious, we rock
in our beds; our rhythms hum
in the stone foundations.
                    We shall have to be careful;
like soldiers who must break step on a bridge.
We stagger our climaxes one by one,
from the basement flat to the attic room,
a pounding of mattresses moves through the house
in a long, multiple, communal orgasm.
The building sighs like a whore house.
We lie in our sheets watching the glow
of the street lights colour the sky; the chimneys
blow their smoke like the mellow exhalations
of post-coital cigarettes.

Neil Rollinson

December 11th

Then I think of you in bed,
your tongue half chocolate, half ocean,
of the houses that you swing into,
of the steel wool hair on your head,
of your persistent hands and then
how we gnaw at the barrier because we are two.

How you come and take my blood cup
and link me together and take my brine.
We are bare. We are stripped to the bone
and we swim in tandem and go up and up
the river, the identical river called Mine
and we enter together. No one's alone.

Anne Sexton (1928 – 1974)

For Desire

Give me the strongest cheese, the one that stinks best;
and I want the good wine, the swirl in crystal
surrendering the bruised scent of blackberries,
or cherries, the rich spurt in the back
of the throat, the holding it there before swallowing.
Give me the lover who yanks open the door
of his house and presses me to the wall
in the dim hallway, and keeps me there until I'm drenched
and shaking, whose kisses arrive by the boatload
and begin their delicious diaspora
through the cities and small towns of my body.
To hell with the saints, with the martyrs
of my childhood meant to instruct me
in the power of endurance and faith,
to hell with the next world and its pallid angels
swooning and sighing like Victorian girls.
I want this world. I want to walk into
the ocean and feel it trying to drag me along
like I'm nothing but a broken bit of scratched glass,
and I want to resist it. I want to go
staggering and flailing my way
through the bars and back rooms,
through the gleaming hotels and the weedy
lots of abandoned sunflowers and the parks
where dogs are let off their leashes
in spite of the signs, where they sniff each
other and roll together in the grass, I want to
lie down somewhere and suffer for love until
it nearly kills me, and then I want to get up again
and put on that little black dress and wait
for you, yes you, to come over here
and get down on your knees and tell me
just how fucking good I look.

Kim Addonizio

The Shipwright's Love Song

Oh, but the lines of her!
The curve and glinting swell –
the *smell*, as fresh as pitch pine,
thick and hot as tar.
Oh, I was launched and splashing in the slipway,
happy to be rudderless
and yawning, mast head
touching to the foam.

Oh, but her skin was salt,
was starred with gasping salt beneath my tongue,
and slowly she came round to me –
bucking and slipping at my touch,
making way in fits and starts
to reach me and be calm.

Later, long before she rocked me into sleep
I saw the seas; saw all of them in one blue ache:
unlandmarked, vast; horizonless.

Jo Bell

Ramadasi

Return
to me, beloved
and take me on your lap.

Undo my braid
stiff
as buffalo horn

and draw your
fingers
through my hair.

Untie my belt, open
the silk cloth
covering my waist,

let my oiled limbs, my
perfumed skin
envelop you

as the rose
swallows
the bee.

Shazea Quraishi

Hidden Rose

Cut open, the inner flesh is pink as nail-polish,
a tissue's lipstick kiss, diluted elderberry in a muslin weave.
Its smooth texture carries a sweet, tart kick.
There's no trace of red in the wood or leaves
and fruit are short-lived on the tree when ripe.
It's as though pomegranates, enchanted into apple-hood,
froze as they changed on first sight of blood.

Wayne Burrows

*The apple variety discovered by William Schulz of Philomath, Oregon, who
named it Airlie Red Flesh, is also widely sold under the name Hidden Rose.
It is a small apple with very distinctive pink interior flesh.*

A Kiss Remembered

Errant, vagrant, the kiss that flew unbidden
the way a swarm will hurtle in, dark on a shining day,
and attach itself, be attached, there on the apple bough,
whole tree vibrating with that force and splendour;

a kiss searching for itself, neither looked for
nor expected, but like the rapt coupling of dragonflies
or the crush of teeth into honeycomb or the first shock
of air to a lung; and still a wound unhealed,

a binary star, inseparable and separate,
shackled in the dance, halves of a gold ring.

MR Peacocke

Gloire de Dijon

When she rises in the morning
I linger to watch her;
She spreads the bath-cloth underneath the window
And the sunbeams catch her
Glistening white on the shoulders,
While down her sides the mellow
Golden shadow glows as
She stoops to the sponge, and her swung breasts
Sway like full-blown yellow
Gloire de Dijon roses.

She drips herself with water, and her shoulders
Glisten as silver, they crumple up
Like wet and falling roses, and I listen
For the sluicing of their rain-dishevelled petals.
In the window full of sunlight
Concentrates her golden shadow
Fold on fold, until it glows as
Mellow as the glory roses.

DH Lawrence (1885 – 1930)

This Morning the Postboy Brought Me a Letter

This morning the postboy brought me a letter
And we exchanged greetings, as we do often:
There was nothing out of the run of things
In what we said to each other; the morning was bright
And cold on the red leaves. As he walked away
Down the path, I noticed the characters
On what I was opening, that hand flew
Into my breast like a bird and I felt
My heart wings beat faster than the thrush
Caught in a snare. Then, as I leant on the porch,
Weak with desire, I also noticed how graceful
The step of the postboy was, how I had never seen
That he was light and delicate as a roebuck,
That the street where my house stands is paradise,
That a slip of paper may contain the whole of creation.

Hilary Davies